M000036143

2000
Classic Designs
for Jewelry

Rings, Earrings, Necklaces, Pendants and More

Richard Lebram

DOVER PUBLICATIONS, INC.
Mineola, New York

Copyright

Copyright © 2008 by Dover Publications, Inc.
All rights reserved.

Bibliographical Note

This Dover edition, first published in 2008, contains seventy-five plates from *Einkaufs-Preisliste für Gold- und Silberwaren,* originally published by Richard Lebram, Berlin, in 1904.

DOVER *Pictorial Archive* SERIES

This book belongs to the Dover Pictorial Archive Series. You may use the designs and illustrations for graphics and crafts applications, free and without special permission, provided that you include no more than ten in the same publication or project. (For permission for additional use, please write to Permissions Department, Dover Publications, Inc., 31 East 2nd Street, Mineola, N.Y. 11501.)

However, republication or reproduction of any illustration by any other graphic service, whether it be in a book or in any other design resource, is strictly prohibited.

Library of Congress Cataloging-in-Publication Data

Lebram, Richard.
  [Einkaufs-Preisliste für Gold- und Silberwaren. Selections]
  2000 classic designs for jewelry : rings, earrings, necklaces, pendants, and more / Richard Lebram.
      p. cm. – (Dover pictorial archive series)
  "This Dover edition, first published in 2008, contains seventy-five plates from Einkaufs-Preisliste für Gold- und Silberwaren, originally published by Richard Lebram, Berlin, in 1904."
    ISBN-13: 978-0-486-46307-0
    ISBN-10: 0-486-46307-9
    1. Jewelry–Catalogs. I. Title. II. Title: Two thousand classic designs for jewelry.
NK7305.L43 2008
739.27–dc22
                                                                    2007041490

Manufactured in the United States of America
Dover Publications, Inc., 31 East 2nd Street, Mineola, N.Y. 11501

Publisher's Note

The allure of jeweled adornments has been so all-encompassing that it is nearly impossible to conceive of any accessory that has not been decorated in some way. In addition to its obvious decorative appeal, jewelry has had great importance throughout history as religious symbols, signs of authority and wealth, and as objects signifying prestige and social status. It has also been used to commemorate social rituals and personal achievements. As in all types of jewelry, the popularity of some items have varied according to the dictates of fashion. One such instance was the pocket watch chain, which had a practical function yet was highly prized for its artistic value. It was often passed down through generations as a family legacy. Other jewelry pieces were intended for purely decorative purposes. These strikingly original adornments were usually the most lavish and elegant, and catered to the constantly changing moods of fashion.

This visual catalog, which reprints a selection of designs from a rare 1904 German work, contains an incredible variety of magnificently crafted jewelry, including bracelets, rings, brooches, lockets, necklaces, chokers, earrings, and many other accessories. Also depicted here are resplendent examples of matching jewelry sets in gold and silver, settings for diamonds and precious stones such as emeralds, rubies, and sapphires, and designs intended for the iridescent color of the opal. This volume of intricate ornamentation reflects the diversity and beauty of the art of jewelry design.

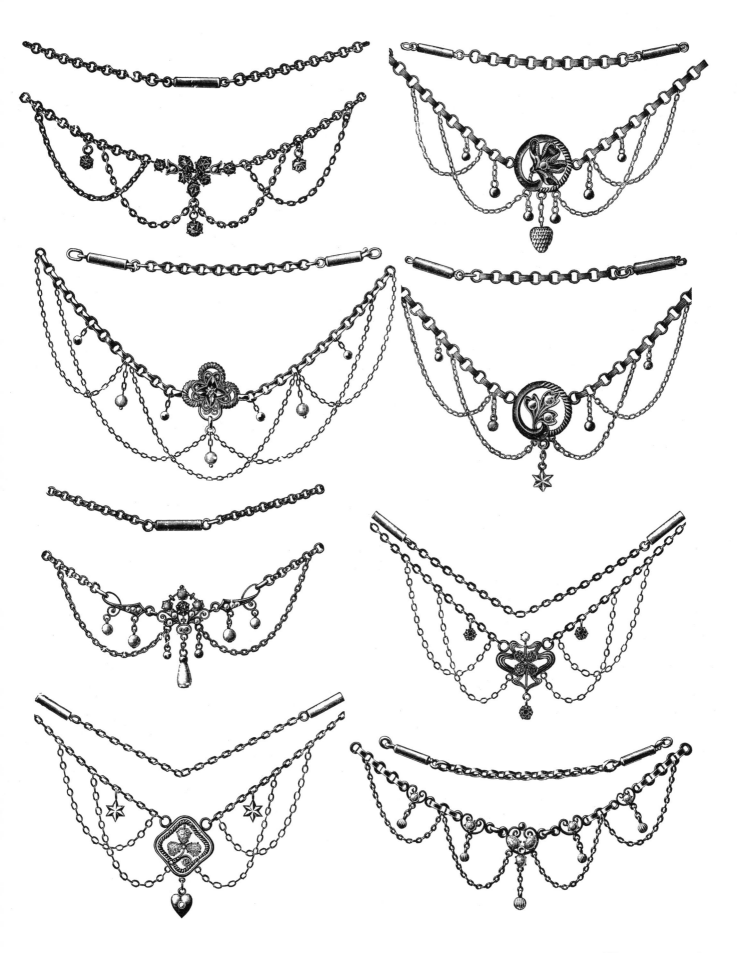

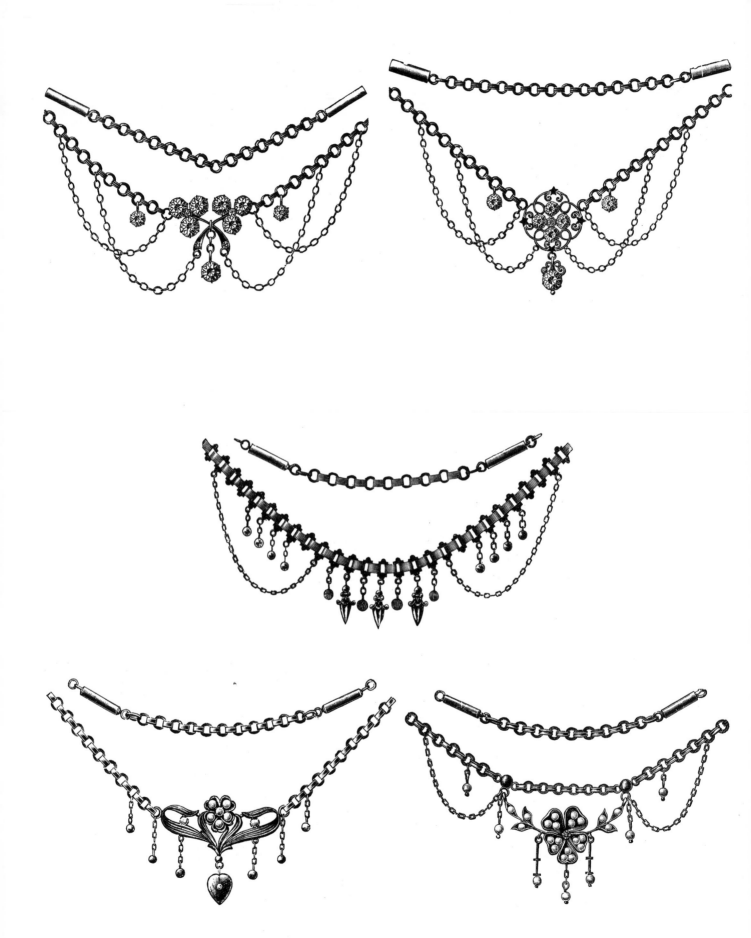

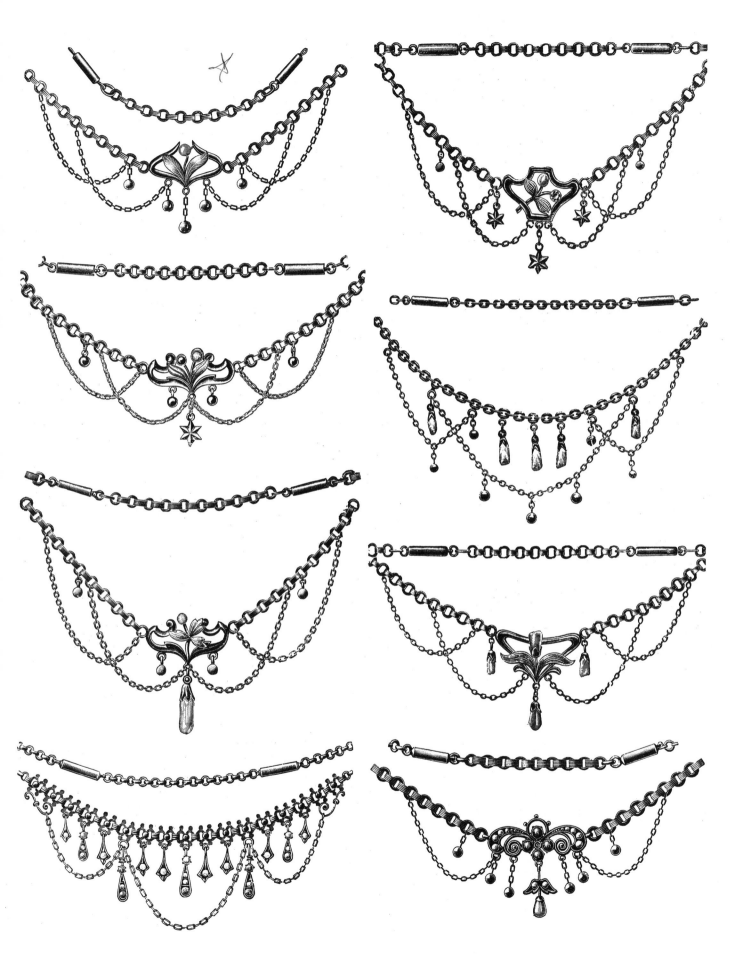

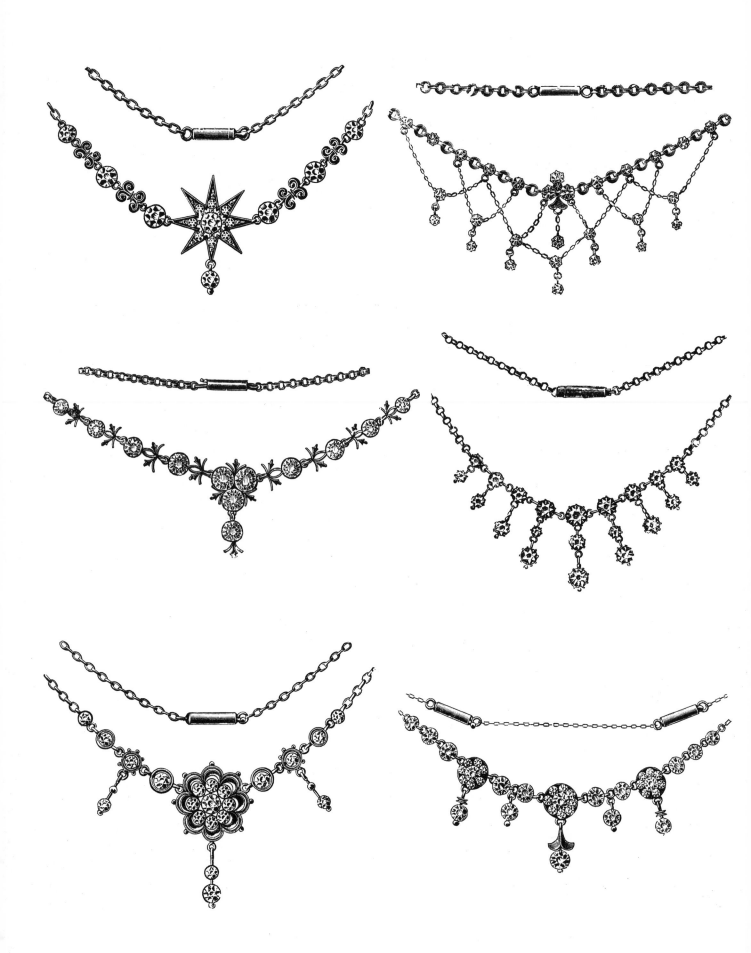

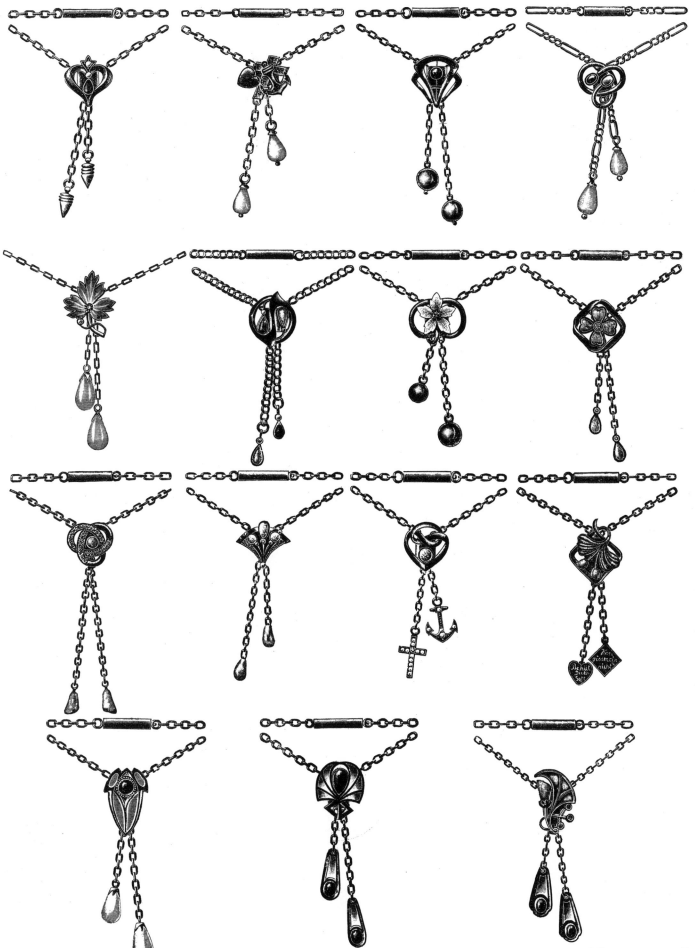

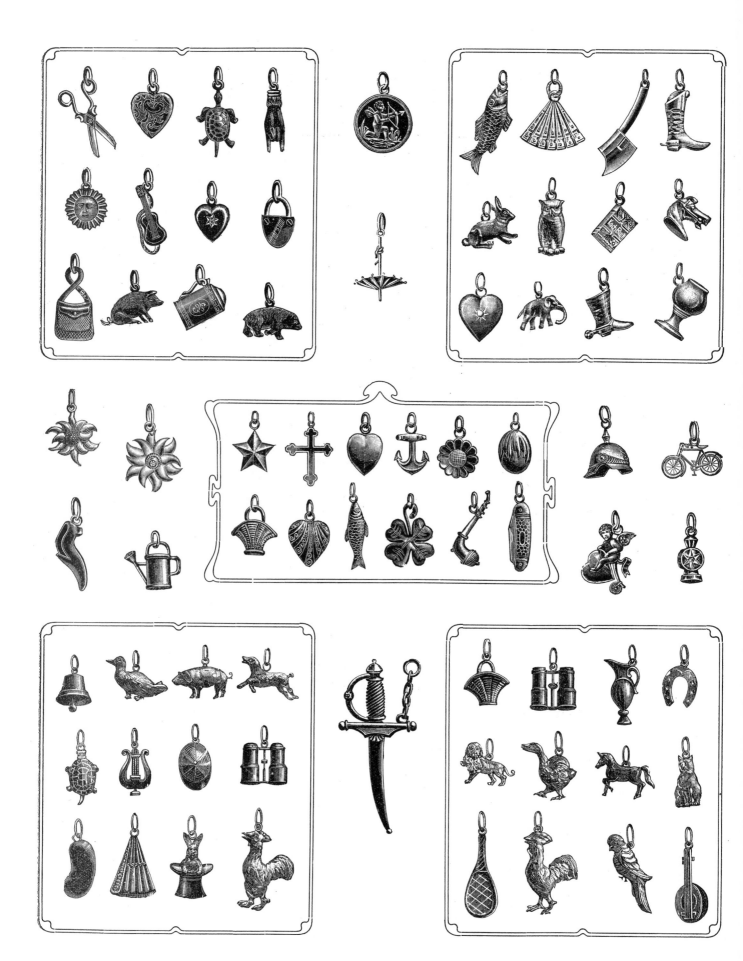

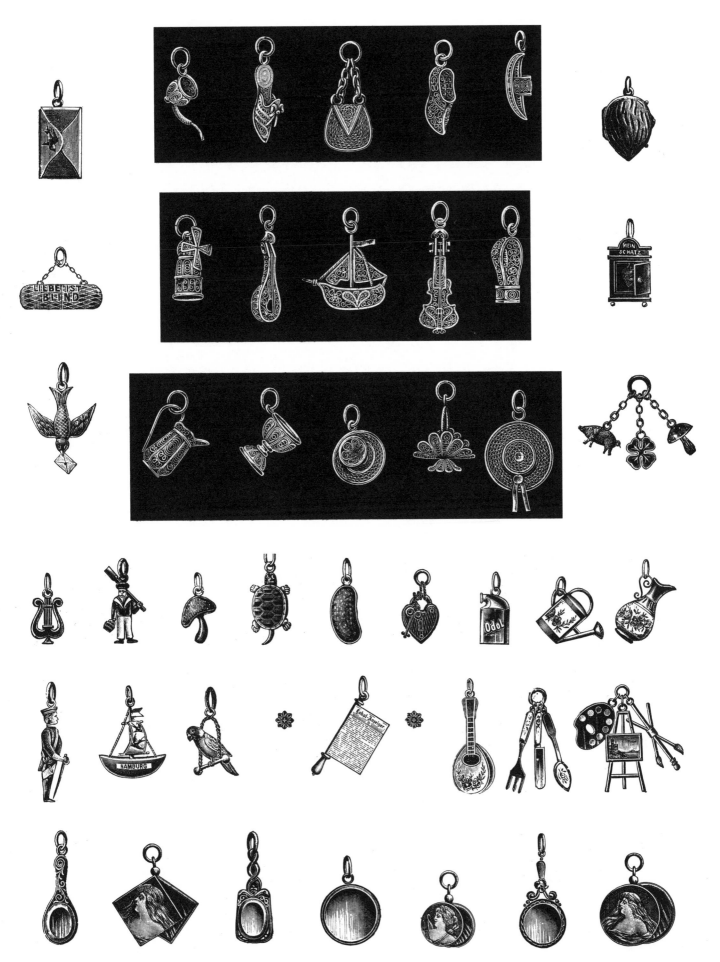

20　Lockets

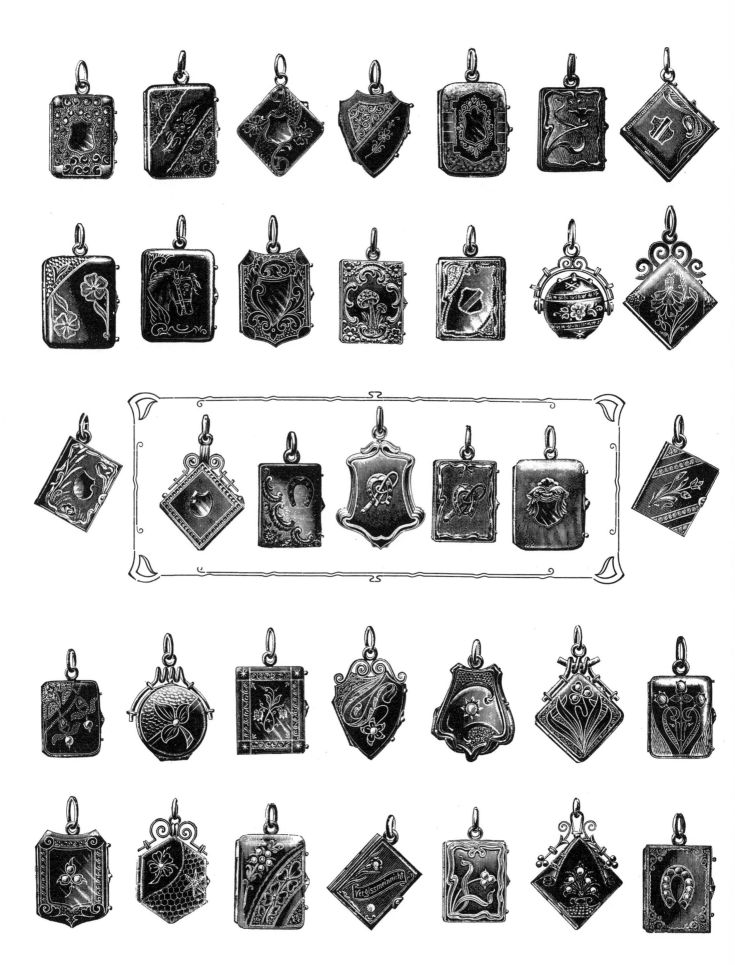

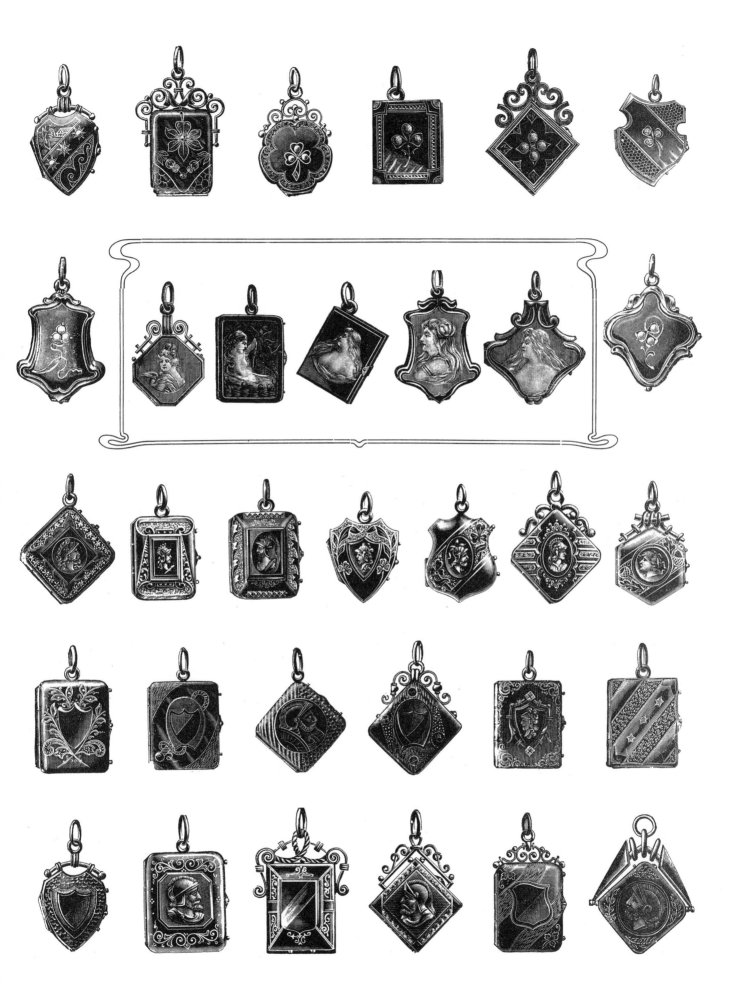

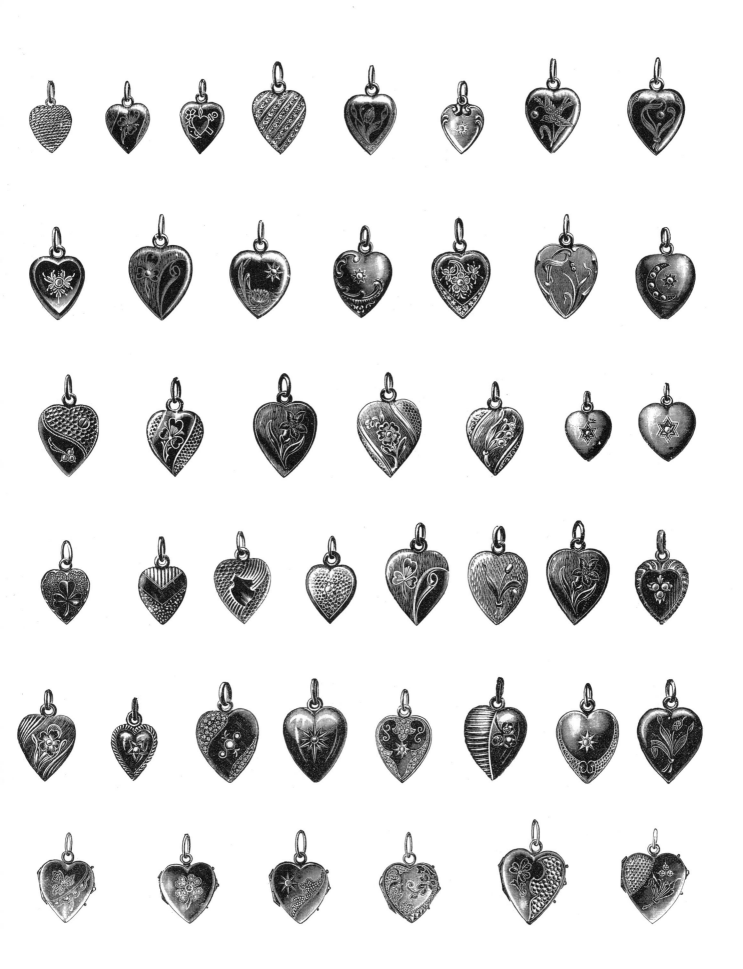

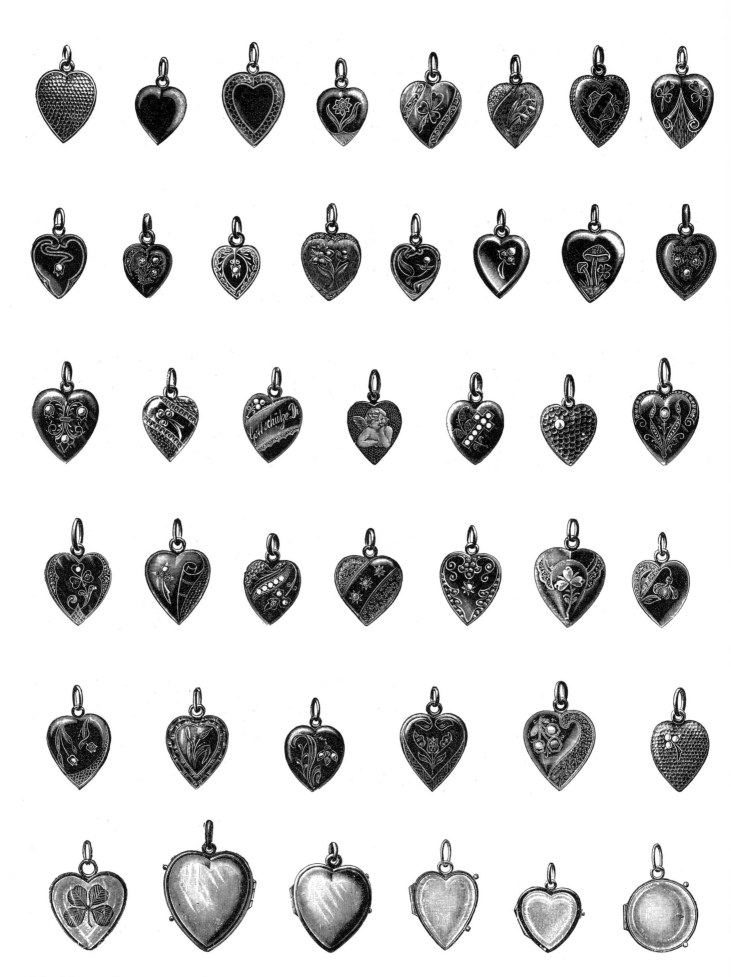

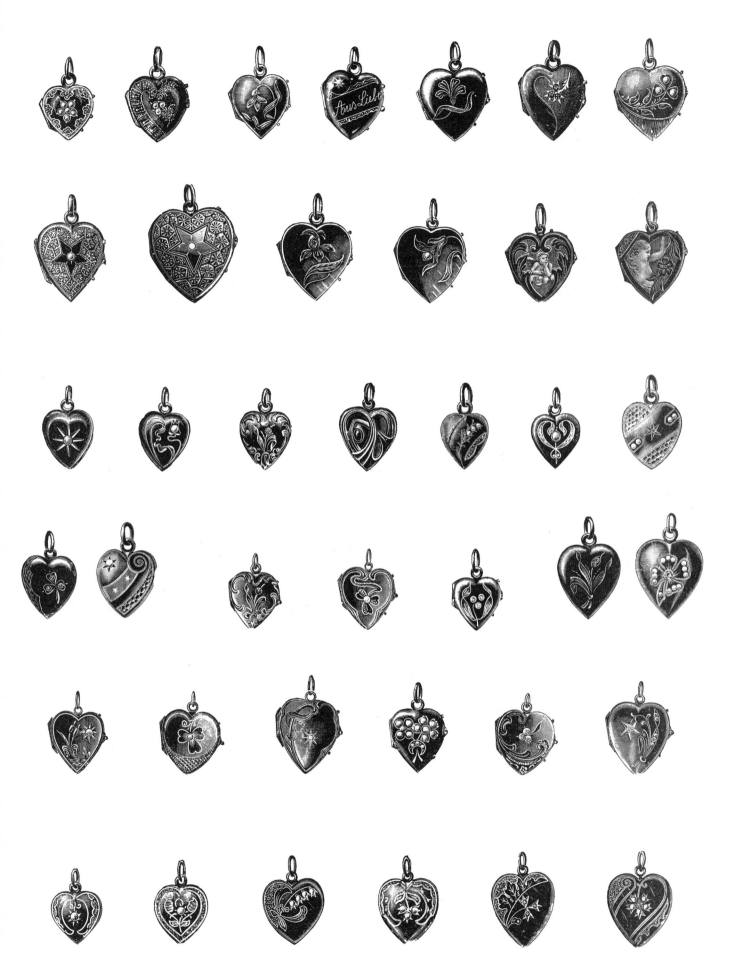

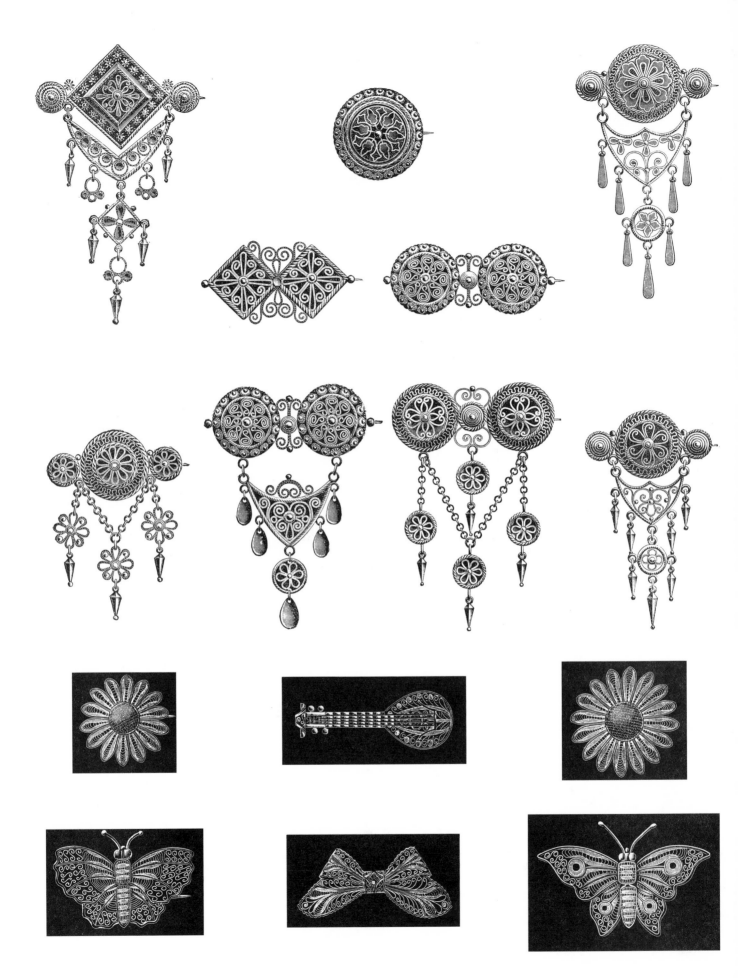

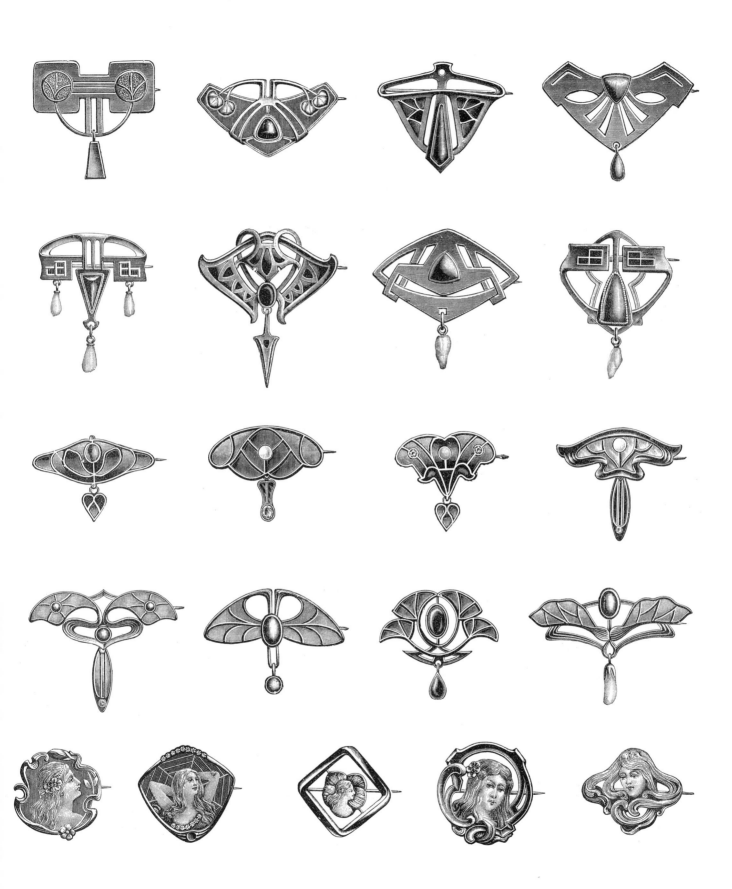

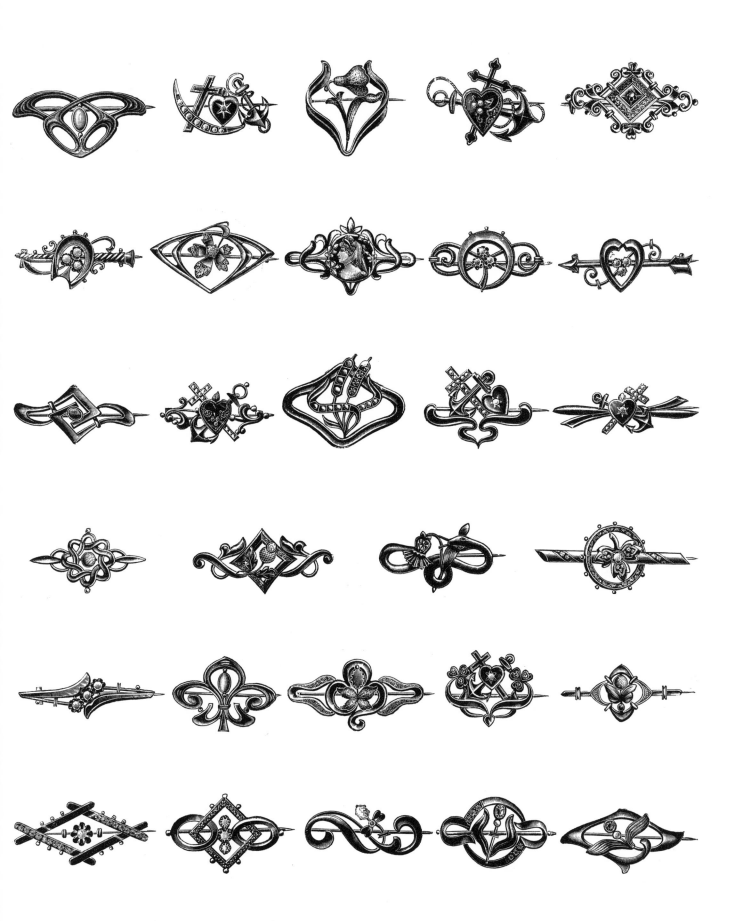

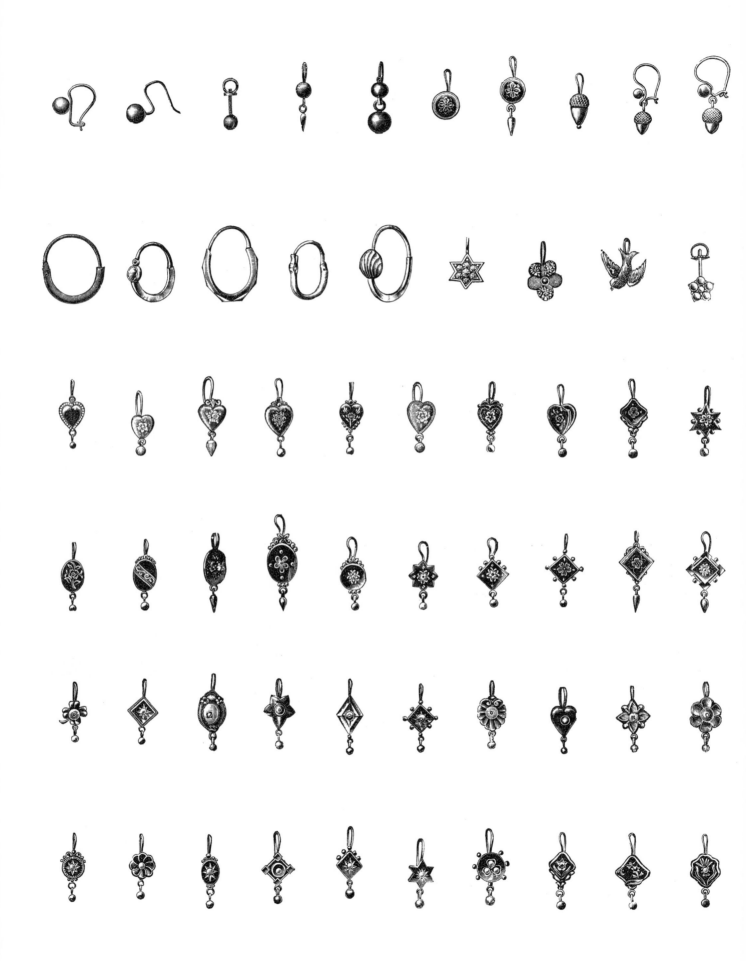

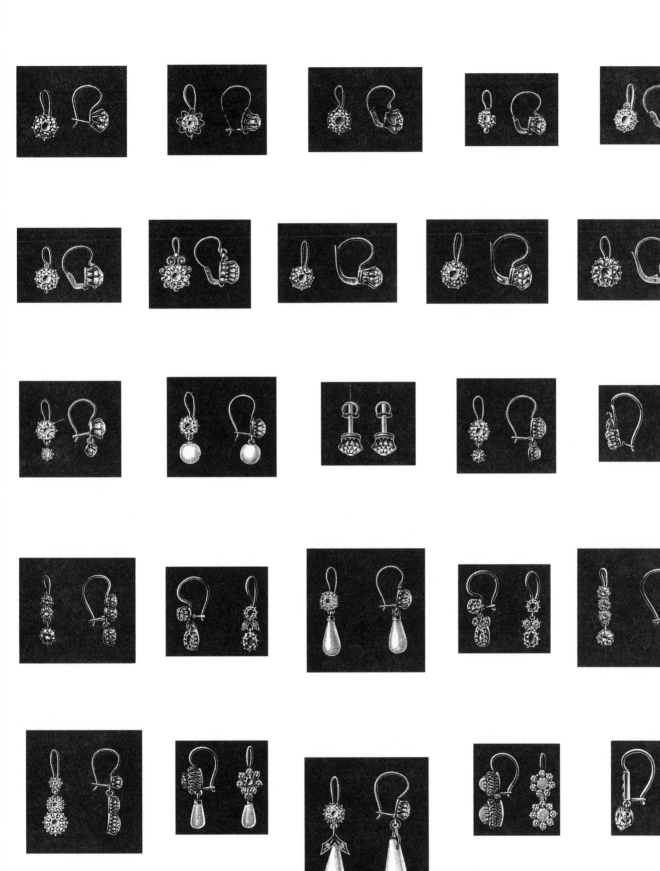

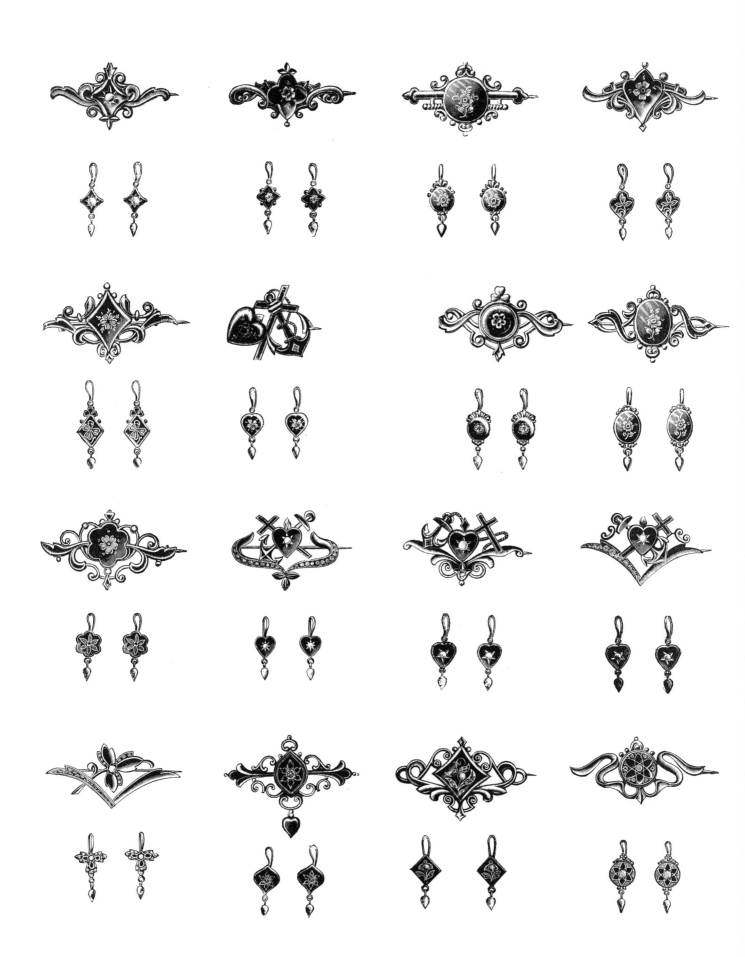

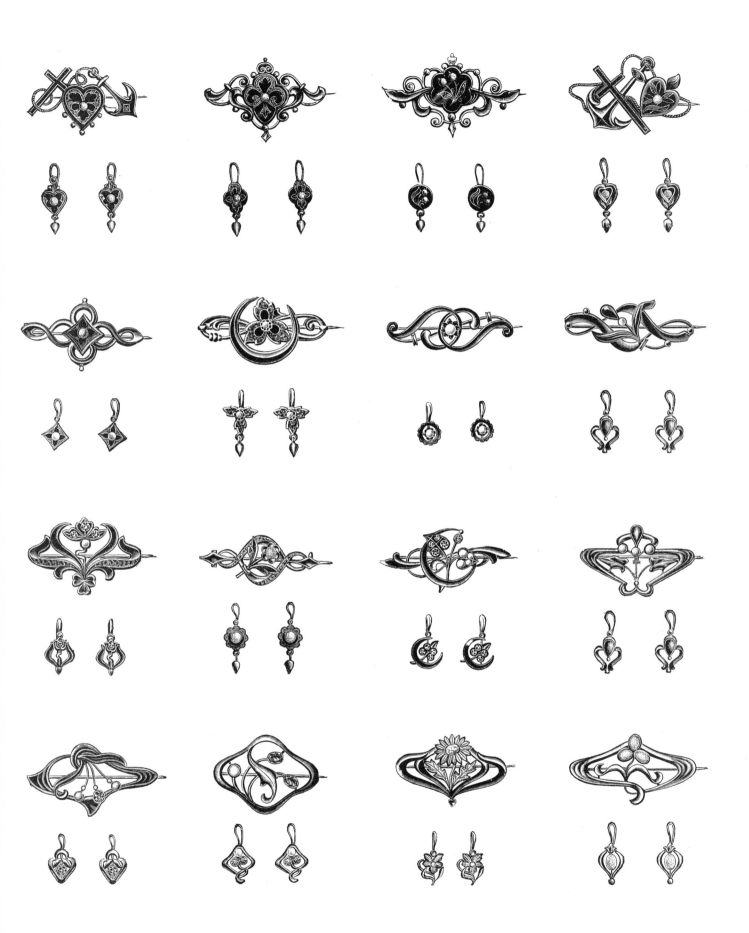

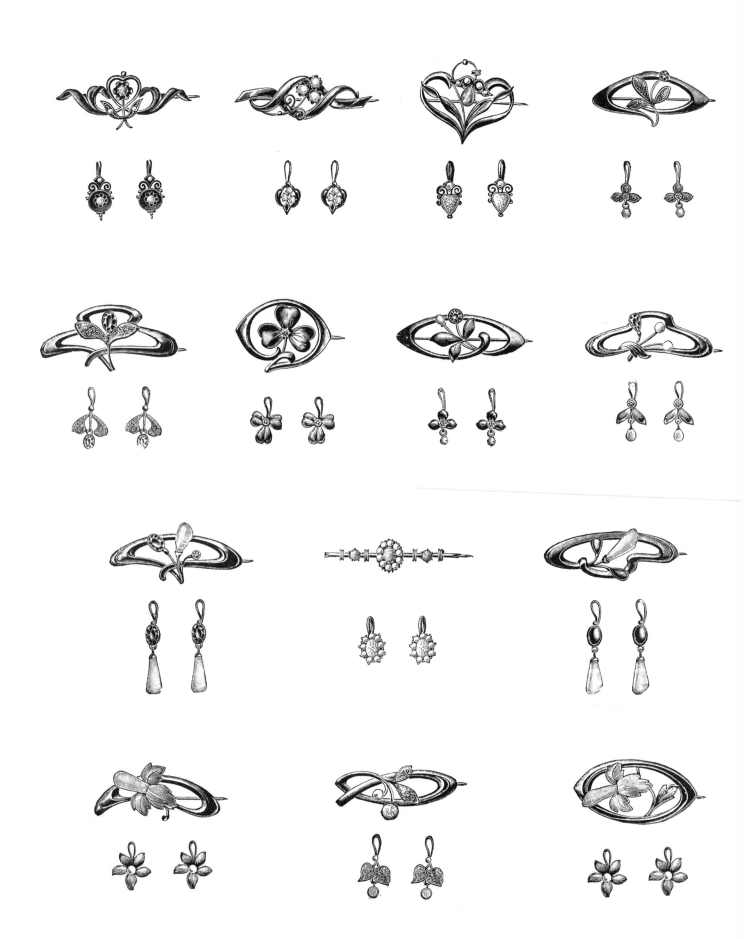

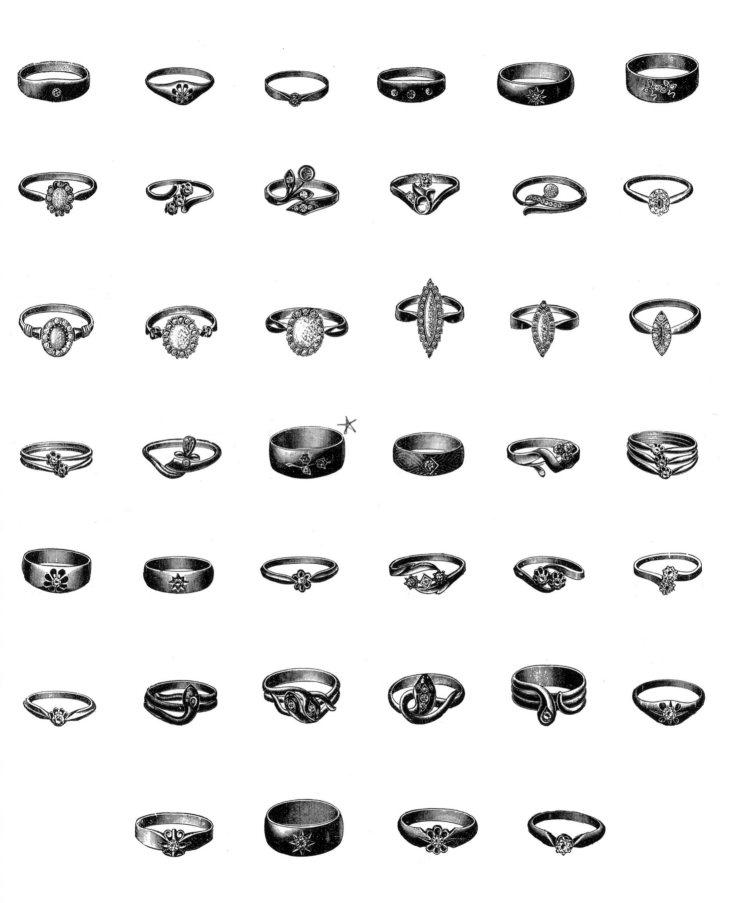

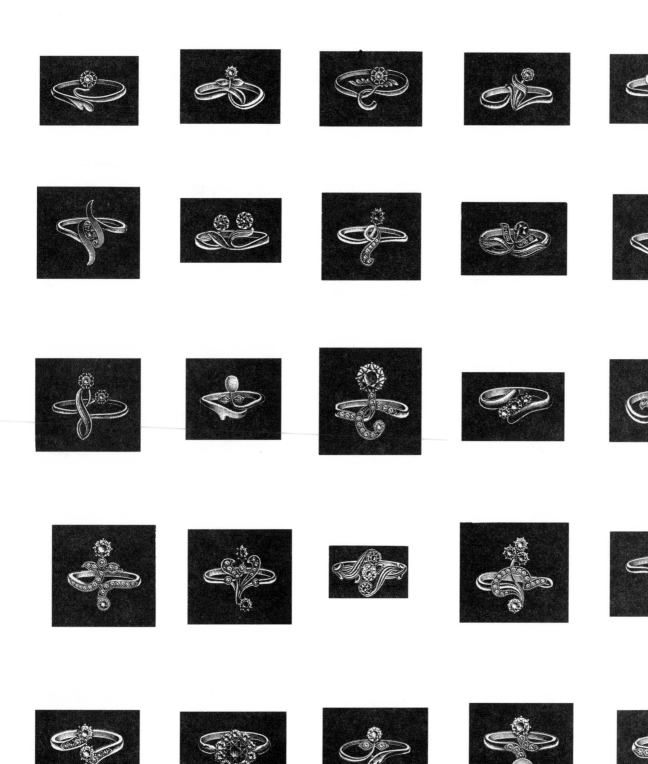

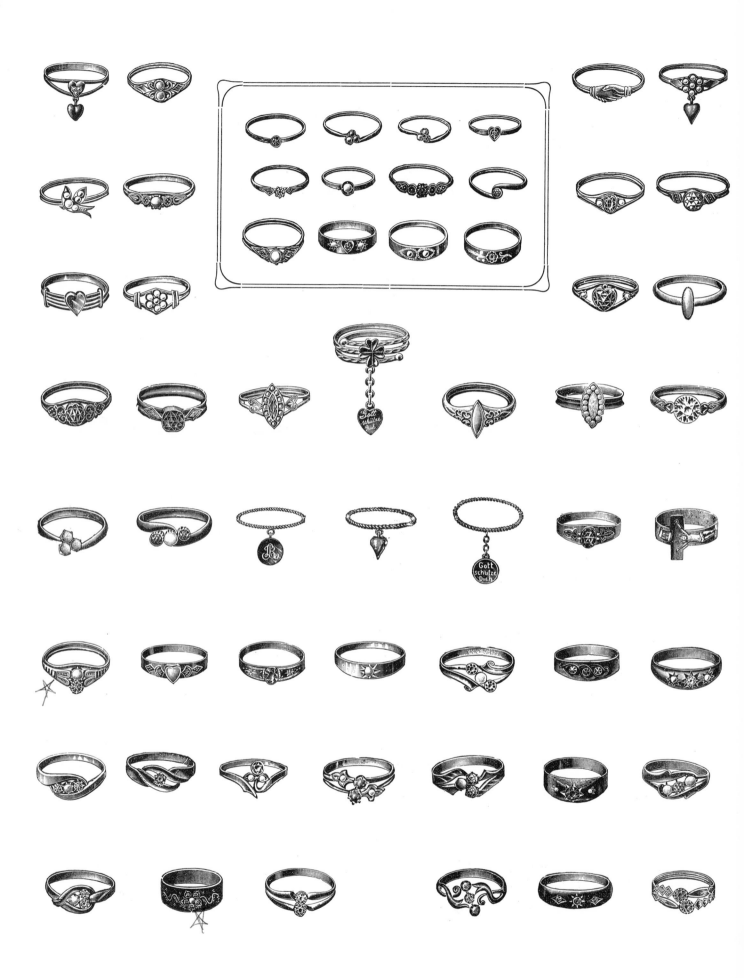

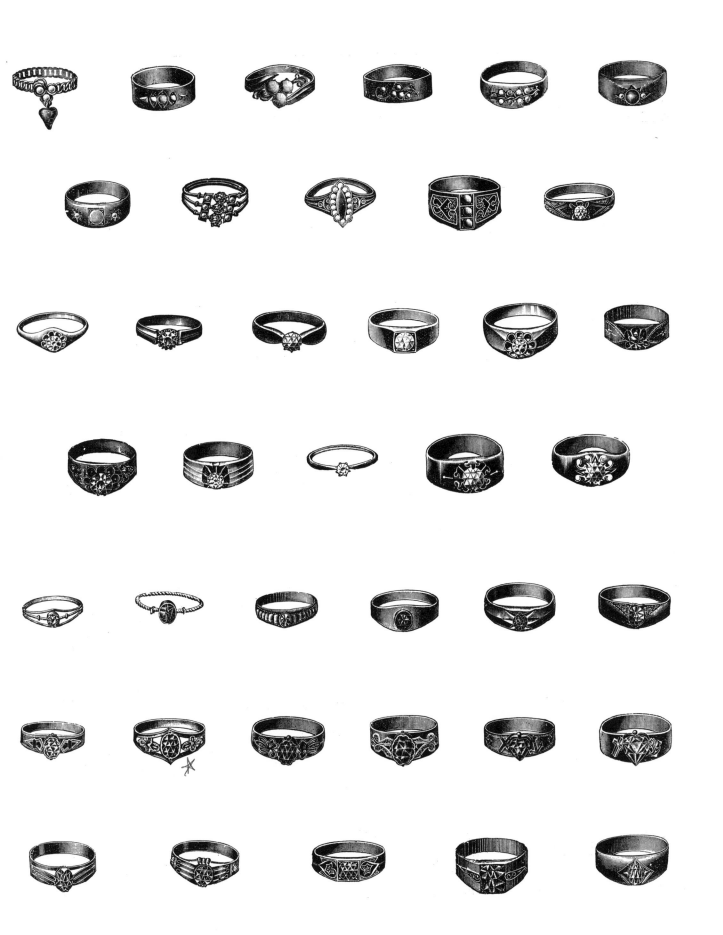

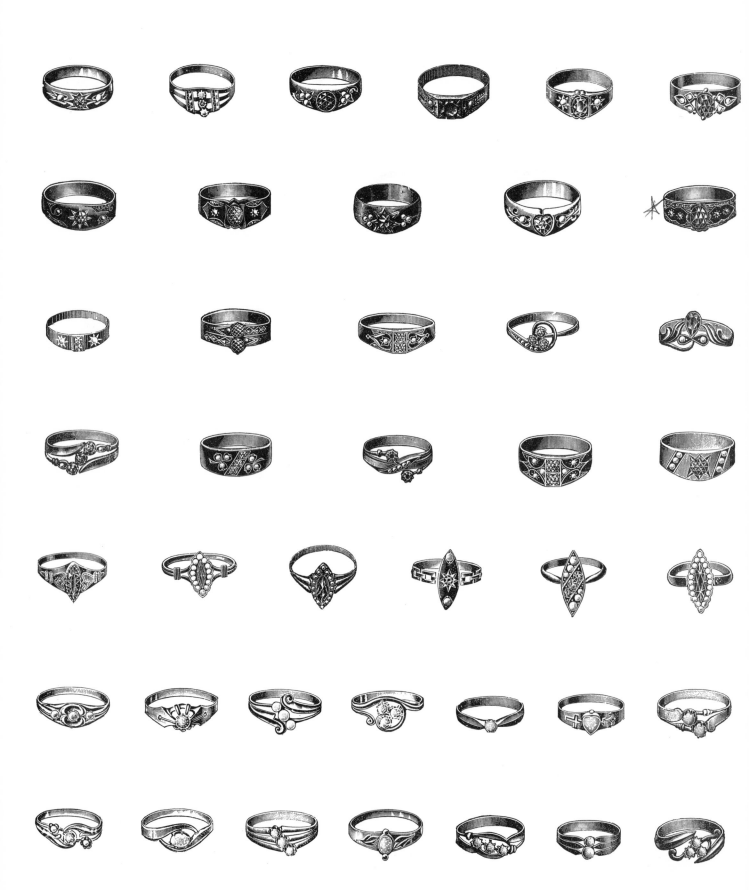

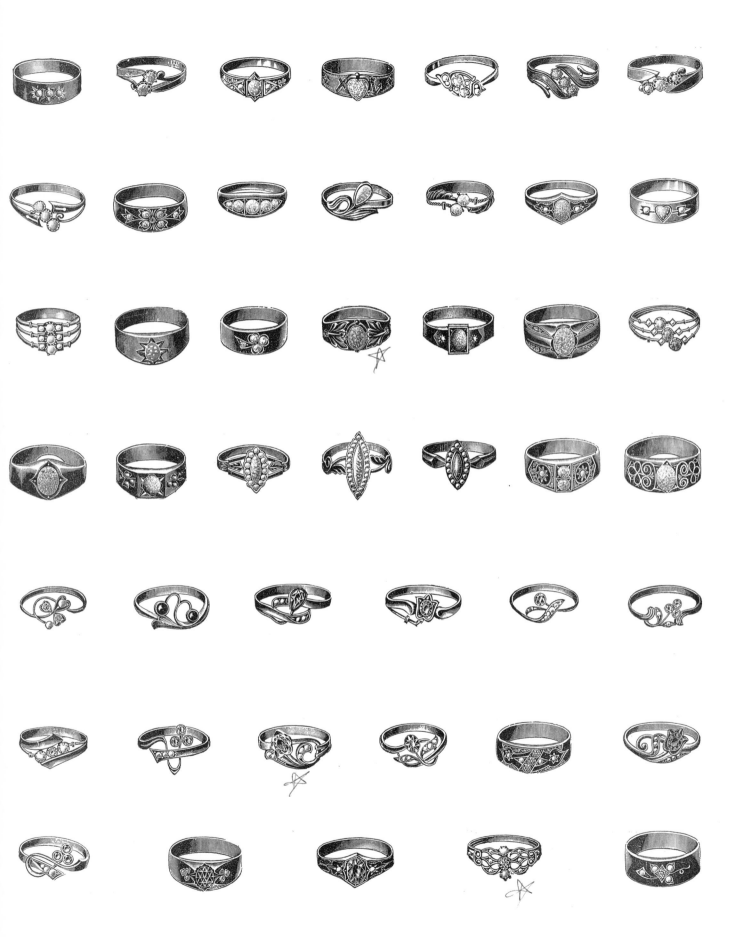

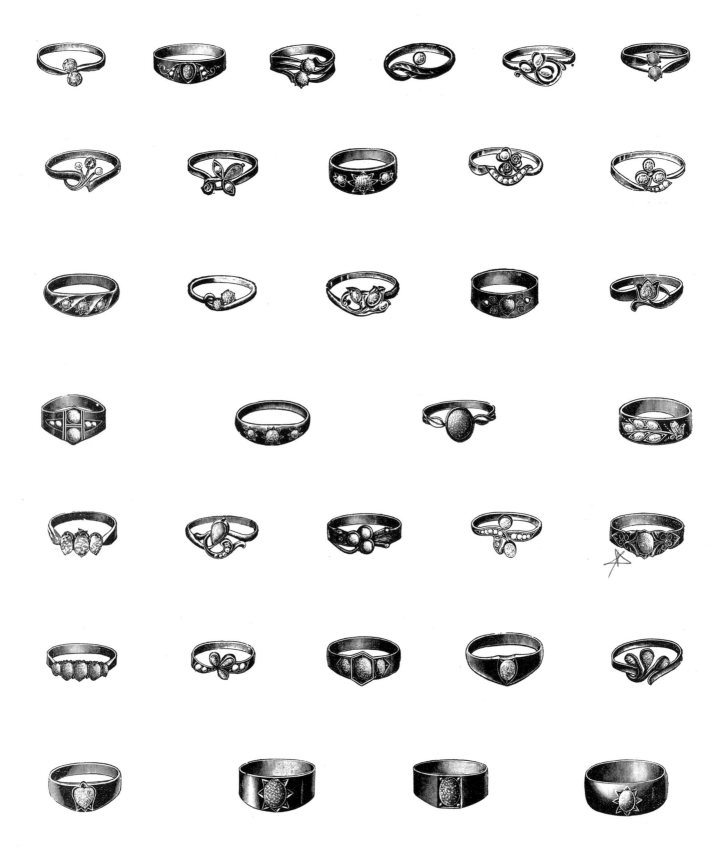

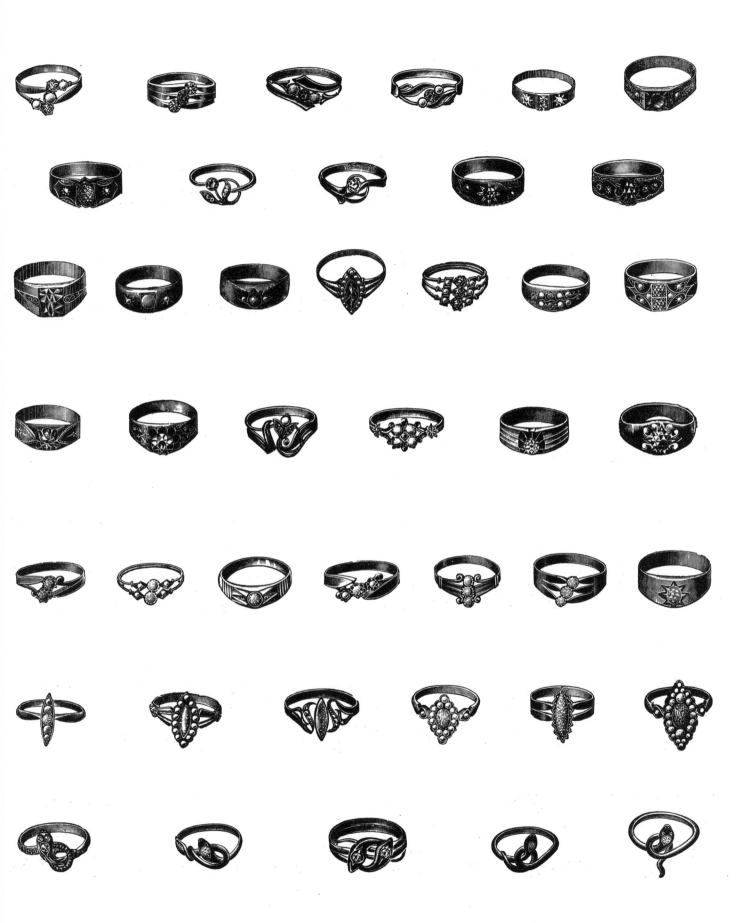

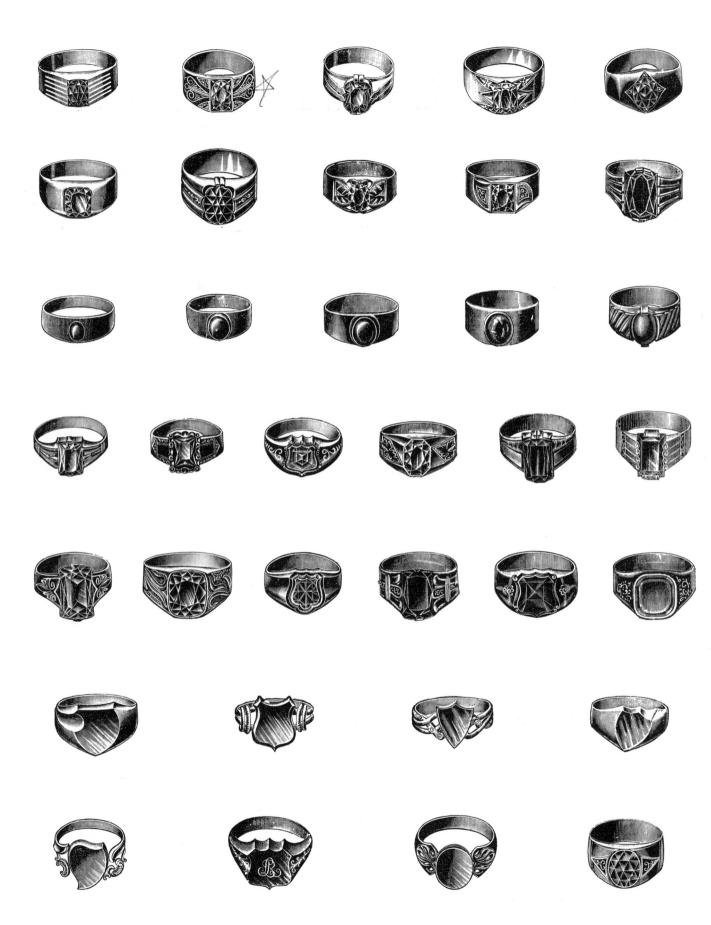

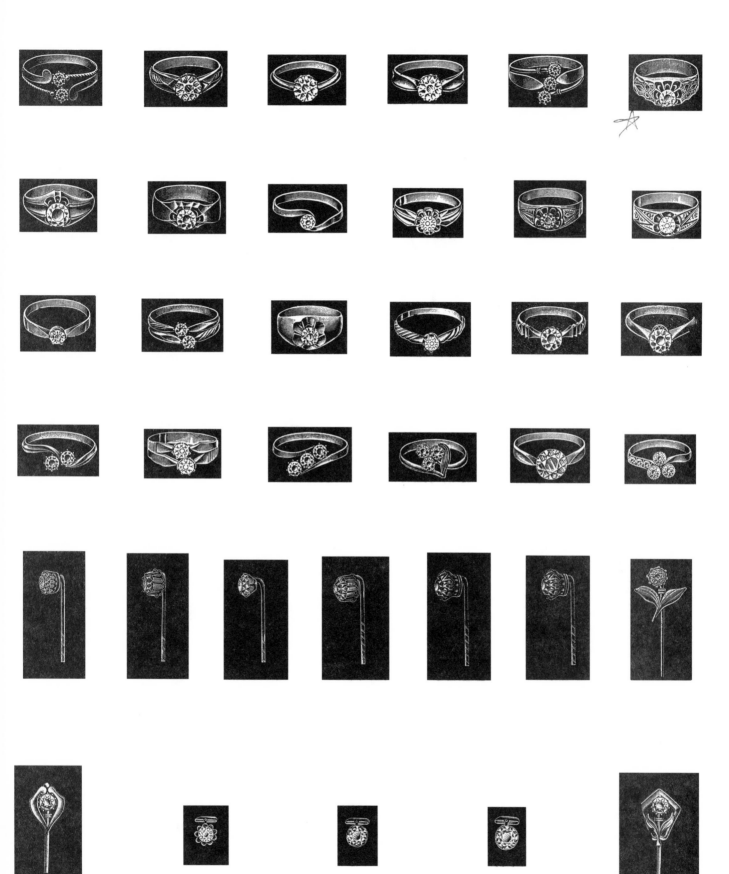

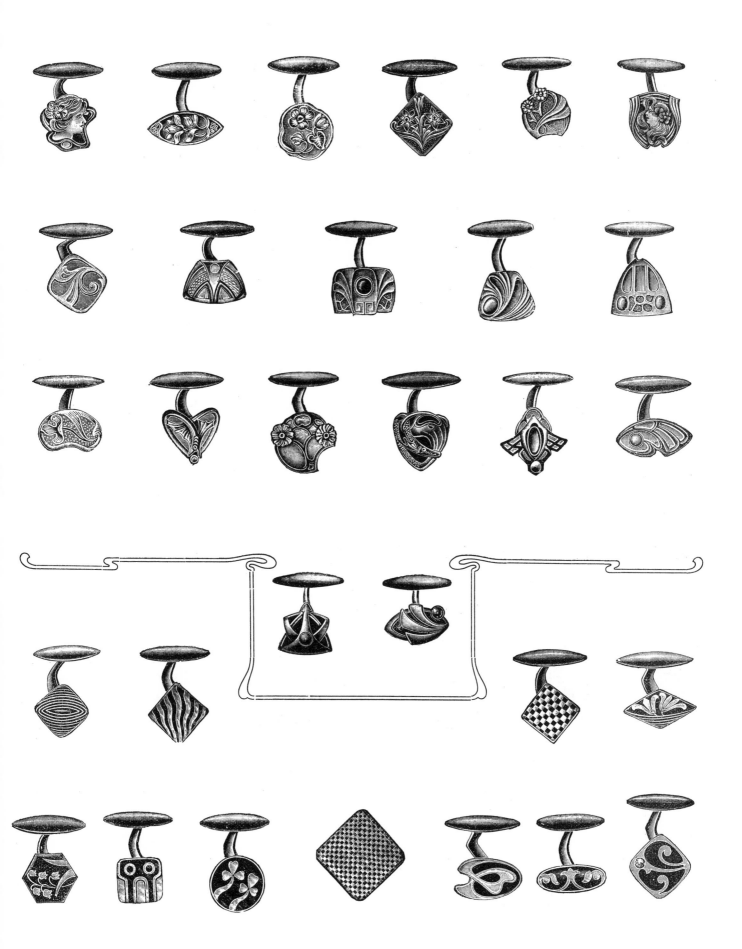

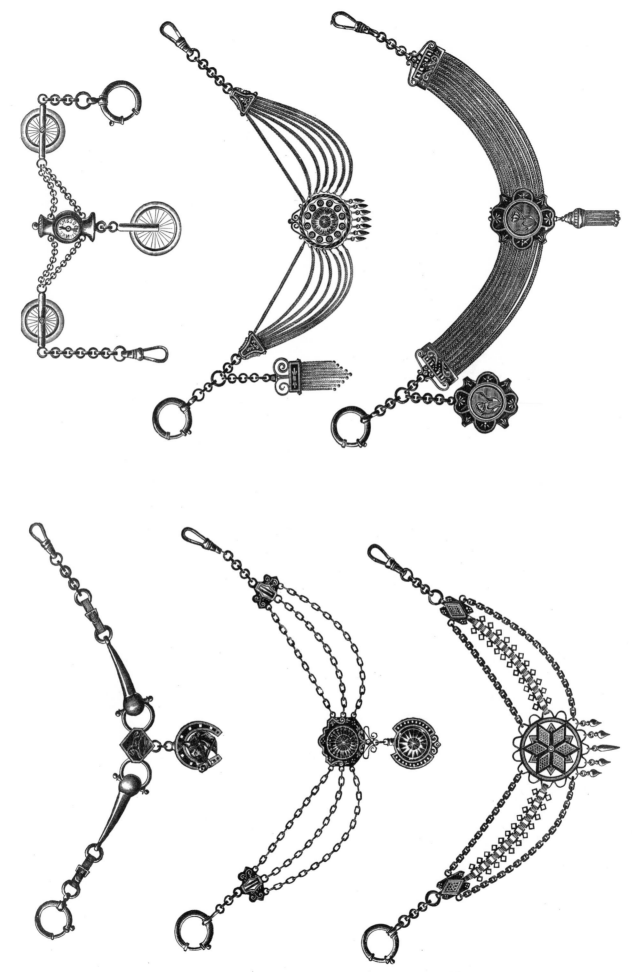

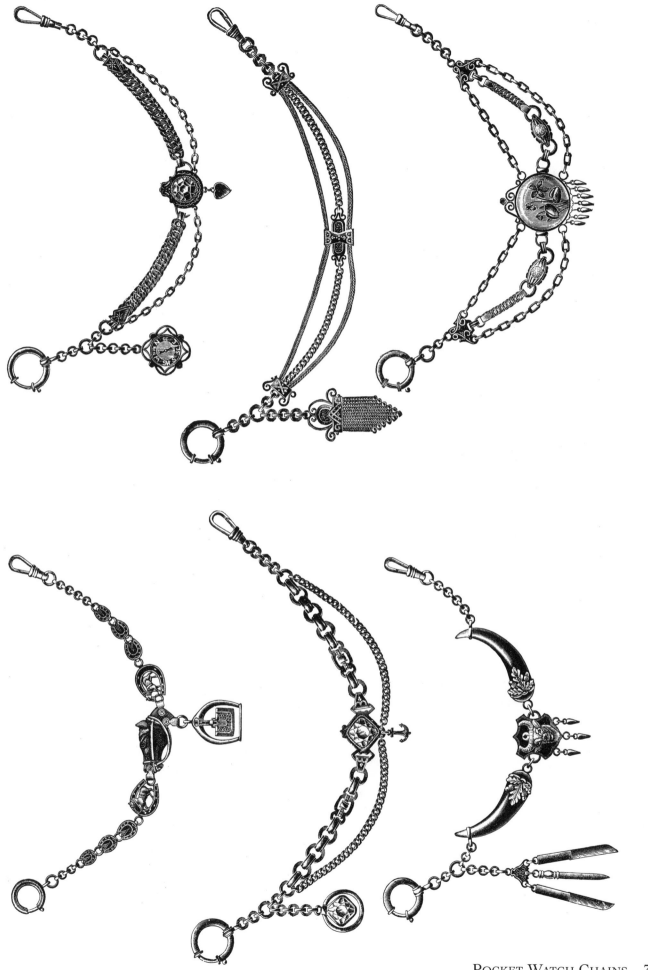

April Wood

bird of paradise blue @ disinfo.net

beth.pohlman @ gmail.com